JANOWSKI GARDENS
Cookbook

"We Grow What We Sell"
and we eat what we grow

by Diane Janowski

New York History Review Press
Elmira, New York

Janowski Gardens Cookbook by Diane Janowski

Published by New York History Review Press, Elmira, New York

For the latest on Janowski Gardens, please visit
www.JanowskiGardens.com

For the latest on New York History Review, please visit
www.NewYorkHistoryReview.com

This book was designed and laid out in Adobe InDesign using typeface
Palatino.

Second edition

ISBN 978-0-615-25495-1

Printed and bound in the United States of America

For Denny,
Because he changed everything....

The Janowski family on the steps of our old homestead on Robinson Street near the foot of Horner Street in Elmira, New York about 1906. From left to right front row: my Grampa, C. Albert, my great-Uncle Henry, my great-Grampa Karl, my great-Aunt Margaret, my great-Grandma Louisa. Back row: my great-Uncle Fritz, my great-Aunt Bertha, her husband Charlie, my great-Uncle Gus, and my great-Aunt Anna. The family built a bigger house around the corner, on Esty Street, soon after this photo was taken.

Cover photograph: The barn sign that greets visitors to Janowski Gardens, built by Uncle Clyde Curren.

Back photograph: If you've been to our farm stand, you've see this sign.

TABLE OF CONTENTS

I have always felt sorry for these horses. This is one big load of celery. The man on top of the load is my Uncle Fritz and the man in the light shirt in the hole is my Uncle Gus. I don't recognize the man in the jacket. After 1910, when our vegetable business really got going, celery, cabbage and parsnips were our specialities. My father says that farmers in this area buried celery in a trench for winter storage. That is what is happening in these photographs.

T his cookbook works well for many different diets. Fat, low-fat, no-fat, and vegetarian. Because every person I know has some dietary restriction, I have written it with choices and substitutions in mind.

In my house, we had to make big dietary changes really quick in September 2002.

I started writing this book in 2001 and I had many recipes already written. Then in June 2002, my life partner, Denny Smith, started experiencing chest pains. He went to his doctor, and after several tests, it was time for the "big test." That one didn't go so good, and on a beautiful fall day in early September, a trip to Guthrie Health Care's Robert Packer Hospital in Sayre, Pennsylvania changed everything. Denny had a clogged artery, and needed angioplasty, and a stent. I was very scared and had a long afternoon in the waiting room.

The next day we met with a nutritionist (the first of three) and she told us what to eat. In respect for Denny, I would also go on his new diet. When we got home, out went the cheese, butter, eggs, red meat, trans fat, and out went my idea of writing this cookbook.

It was very hard to cook (and eat) during the first weeks because of the possibility of a recurrence. I wasn't going to let that happen again – ever. We ate a lot of rice and beans the first month. On this new diet, both of us discovered that we regularly have hypoglycemia, and the high oxalate levels in the heart diet aggravated Denny's kidneys – not to mention the prescribed heart diet was very bland and not very interesting. We were going to have to figure out a better way to eat. In came nutritionist #2. She gave us some new ideas and the hopes of introducing some foods back into our diet. Two eggs a week are ok, 95% ground beef is good, fat-free products work great in recipes, extra rice and vegetables to replace meat, using lots of bold herbs and spices, and learning to make substitutions helped us a lot. I had to rethink my way of cooking and come up with ways that both of us would enjoy our food. I'm good at that.

So anyway, I started rewriting my cookbook – this time in a new way. In my household - I should not eat soy or foods in the cabbage family (my scary afternoon at Guthrie damaged my thyroid leaving me with thyroid disease) and Denny should avoid fat, cholesterol, and oxalate-rich foods. And, nobody should eat trans fats. We have a "No foods list" stuck on our refrigerator, and we balance everything we eat – as Denny always says, "Everything in moderation." We follow the Food and Drug Administration's guidelines of less than 20 grams of saturated fat per day. Most days we do much better than that. The biggest change in our house is that we read EVERY food label.

Here it is 6 years later - we are still sticking to a heart-healthy diet and lifestyle. My goal is, and has been, to include as much flavor as possible to whatever we eat. I never make meals the same way twice, I cut vegetables into interesting shapes, I use all kinds of fun-looking pasta, I vary herbs and spices in recipes, and most especially, I am as absolutely creative as I can be in the kitchen. I want both of us to enjoy our food and the rest of our lives.

So anyway, I have not been to culinary school; I don't mince, or chop very well; I am dangerous with kitchen knives; pots always boil over, measurements aren't perfect; and I make a big mess in the kitchen. So what? - I still like to cook. I definitely encourage substitutions for what you don't like, can't have, or need more of. I do know what I like and what fresh vegetables and fruits are good for me and Denny, and I'm sharing our recipes.

First parcel of land that my great-great grampa purchased in 1873. Today it is the area of our strawberry patch. Photo 2005.

OUR HISTORY

If you know me, you know that history is involved in everything I do - so history in a cookbook is not unusual and this book is full of it. I have traced my branch of the Janowski family back to Racek Janovsky in 1279AD in Pajrek, Klatovy, Czechoslavakia. Around 1500, we moved to West Prussia, later called East Germany, and since World War II, Poland.

Frederick Janowski (my great-great grandfather) and his family waited until the Franco-Prussian War was over in 1871 to come to America. They immigrated from Tuchel, Germany (now Tuchola, Poland) in May 1872 on the *Bark Louis*.

My ancestors came to Elmira, New York and found a place to live on Robinson Street near the foot of Horner Street. There, the family picked fruit in the orchards for the rest of the summer and fall. They saved enough money to purchase their first parcel (9 acres) of farmland along Esty and Robinson Streets in the spring of 1873. The first parcel is where our strawberry patch is today (photo on opposite page).

Here is a photo of my great-Grampa Karl waiting for the end of the Franco-Prussian War so that he could emigrate to the U.S.

Frederick, his wife Louisa, and their children Gustave, William, Karl (my great-grampa), Daniel, Johannes, and Julia worked the farm. Frederick died in 1885 and the farm was left to his son Gustave who died shortly thereafter passing the estate to his brothers and sisters.

As the siblings grew older and eventually died, the farm was left to the seven children of Karl (including Gus, my grampa Albert,

We came over on this boat - the *Bark Louis* in May 1872.

and Fritz who continued the business calling themselves the "Janowski Brothers" and provided many Elmira grocery stores and restaurants with fresh vegetables. Uncle Gus purchased more acres between 1910 and 1915 after the family moved around the corner on Esty Street. There were probably 50 acres all together (today we have around 25 acres and use about 20). As the neighborhood grew, Gus sold many acres and they became the lots on Robinson Street facing Brand Park, and the lots on the southside of Esty Street and northside of Liberty Street. Eventually, Albert was the last of the three brothers, and he and his sons continued the business as "C. Albert Janowski & Sons." After his death in 1976, his sons Robert and Paul formed "Janowski Gardens." I am Robert's daughter, and have continued the family tradition by helping on the farm for many years. Good family friends including Denny Smith, Scott Tolbert, and Jim Freeman also contribute their time to the helping the family operation. My brother, Tom, worked on the farm until he graduated from college and now lives in Rochester, New York.

Many residents remember the years, before her retirement, that my mother, Hildegard Janowski ran the vegetable stand behind the house. She was born in East Germany, but her family moved to West Germany before the end of World War II. She immigrated to the United States in 1957, and became a U.S. citizen in 1962. Therefore, I am a first-generation American on my mother's side. Before my mom, my grandmother, Loretta, worked in the stand.

I've done a lot of local family genealogy using the Chemung County census at the Steele Memorial Library in Elmira and found that my last name was *usually* misspelled - Jenusky, Genasky, Janawski, Joloski, Jenosky, Jalowski, Janosky, Jenowski, Jenuski, Janowskie, Jamowfki, Janwoski, Joneski, Geneski, Gineski, Janiesky, Jannuaski, Janeszka, Jaeniski, Janaski, Janoska, Jenofsky, Janowsko, Janovska, Janoosky,

Jonowsky, Jannowski, and Jinosky. My favorite misspelling, though, is Chanowski.

It was probably very difficult being a census taker at the turn of the 20th century, but it also makes it very difficult to do family research today.

Today's homegrown specialties of Janowski Gardens include sweet corn, cabbage, squash, potatoes, beans, strawberries, lettuce, Swiss chard, onions, collards, tomatoes, eggplant, peppers, and melons.

We have two barns. In this book I refer to them as "left barn" and "right barn." This is our left barn in different years - top circa 1910, bottom in 2005. We have had our farm stand here under the low roof since the 1972 flood. The right barn (not shown here) was built within a few years of the left one.

A stack of baskets waiting to be filled, circa 2006.

Soups and Sauces

There are many ingredients and appliances that I can't cook without: Olivio™ margarine, all flavors of McIlhenny's™ Tabasco sauces, Tony Chachere's (Tony's™) Creole seasoning, Tiger Sauce™, Louisiana pecans, fat-free half & half, tons of black pepper, low-fat chicken sausage, vegetable bouillon, and Creole mustard. Denny and I love lots of flavors and spices in our food. I also love my Ronco™ Food Dehydrator and my Braun™ Hand Blender.

Here is my father, Robert, at the Elmira Wisner Market. Farmers' Markets are very hard work. It takes us three days to get ready to go to market.

Hurricane Ivan Soup

September 17, 2004 the day remnants of Ivan hit Elmira

Perfect for really rainy days – don't waste this on a good day

6 medium potatoes - cut in chunks
1 onion – minced
olive oil
¼ cup red peppers - diced
1 carrot – sliced
1 rib of celery – sliced
3 tablespoons butter
1 link cooked and sliced chorizo or andouille sausage (chicken
    sausage is great)
2 cups chicken or vegetable stock
2 tablespoons chopped fresh parsley
Creole spices (our favorite is Tony's) to taste or salt and pepper
Tabasco
1 pinch dried thyme or 1 bigger pinch fresh thyme
a little bit of jalapeño for some zip

*Two procedures take place at the same time.

1. In large pot, place potatoes in about 1½ inches water. Bring to boil, cover and reduce heat to medium-low and cook for about 20-25 minutes. At that point, potatoes will be mostly done. Mash potatoes in the pot with the water – but leave them kind of lumpy. Lightly season with Creole spices or salt and pepper.

2. In a large frying pan, sauté onions and red and jalapeño peppers in olive oil until onions are translucent. Then, add carrot and celery. After 5 minutes add 3 tablespoons butter and sausage and mushrooms. Sauté 5 minutes more.

Then, in the potato pot add the sautéed vegetables and sausage, chicken stock, parsley, thyme, and a dash of Tabasco. Bring to a boil, then cover, reduce to simmer for ten minutes more. Enjoy with fresh bread.

Celery was one of our specialities. Pictured here, circa 1919, in our right barn doorway, from left to right is great-Aunt Margaret, cousins Mildred and Eleanor Schiller, and great-Grandma Louisa posing with some of our best celery. Below is my Grampa pulling a wood wagon with Chippy, Uncle Henry's dog, on top, circa 1945.

Mushroom Onion Soup
A comfort food with a twist

½ pound mushrooms - finely chopped

Juice of ½ lemon

2 tablespoons butter or margarine

½ onion - minced

2 cups milk

1 ½ cups chicken broth

½ teaspoon freshly ground pepper

Salt to taste

2 teaspoons cornstarch dissolved in 2 tablespoons cold water

1 teaspoon fresh parsley - chopped

1 teaspoon minced garlic

1 pinch American saffron or turmeric for a golden color

1 pinch dried thyme

In bowl, mix mushrooms with lemon juice. Over low heat, melt butter in large skillet and add minced onion and garlic, sauté until soft (I always add a little water while sautéing, so I don't need as much oil). Add mushrooms and cook, stirring frequently, until liquid is completely evaporated (about 10 minutes).

Add milk, thyme, saffron, chicken broth and pepper. Bring to a boil. Reduce heat, cover, and simmer 10 minutes. Add dissolved cornstarch and simmer 5 more minutes (or until thickened). Adjust seasoning and ladle into serving bowls. Garnish with chopped parsley. 4-6 servings.

For any recipe in this book that calls for milk you really can use whatever you like - whole, skim, soy, cream, half & half, or fat-free half & half. Any recipe that calls for mayonnaise or sour cream you may easily substitute low-fat, no- fat, yogurt, or soy versions. We do like Olivio margarine for a buttery flavor with no trans fats.

Zucchini Soup
Surprisingly good.

2 tablespoons butter or margarine

2 medium zucchinis - chopped

1 onion - chopped

2 cloves garlic - minced

1 teaspoon curry powder

salt to taste

1 teaspoon white pepper

4 cups chicken or vegetable broth

½ cup milk

1 pinch dried basil

1 pinch dried parsley

Dash of tabasco

Melt butter in pot. Stir in zucchini, garlic, onion. Sauté 10 minutes. Add curry, salt and pepper, milk, and 2 cups of broth. Heat until boiling, then puree - or partially puree with a hand blender right in the pot - Denny likes it a little bit chunky. Stir in remaining 2 cups of broth. Reheat and serve.

Last summer a customer asked me what he could do with a bunch of those big, late summer zucchinis. Otherwise known as "yardstick squash."

I said, "Oh, yes. Gather them up and get yourself a card table. Then go down by the road and lay the zucchinis on the table. Then put up a sign that says, 'Free' and walk away."

Above, corn fields, circa 1916. Above from left to right: great-Uncle Fritz, great-Uncle Gus, Rex the dog, Grampa, and two unknown (to me) men.

Below, me and Denny picking corn in 2004.

Cabbage Portobella Soup
Definitely good

½ small cabbage – shredded
½ onion - minced
8 baby portobella or brown mushrooms – sliced
1 can cream of mushroom soup
Some milk or cream
3 tablespoons chopped fresh parsley
½ tablespoon minced garlic
Pinch of marjoram or thyme
Vegetable bouillon powder or salt and pepper to taste
Tabasco to taste

In big pot, add 1½ inches water and bring to boil. Add cabbage and parsley. Cover and reduce to a gentle boil for 10 minutes If you prefer a creamy soup - use a hand blender at this point and puree cabbage slightly - right in the pot. Add mushrooms. After 10 more minutes, add the cream of mushroom soup and enough milk to make a consistency that you like. Add Tabasco, garlic, spices, and seasonings to taste. Simmer 5 minutes more. Serve with your favorite bread.

Bin of onions in our farm stand, 2005.

Chunky Cream of Turkey Soup

A nice blend of fresh flavors

¼ onion - chopped

2 celery ribs - chopped

2 tablespoons butter or margarine

1 tablespoon minced garlic

1 teaspoon thyme

1 teaspoon rosemary - crushed

2 cups corn

2 cups cooked diced turkey breast meat

2 cups chicken broth

¼ cup flour

2 cups milk

1 squirt Worcestershire sauce

salt and black pepper to taste

ground cayenne pepper to taste

In a big pot, sauté onions, celery, and garlic in butter. When onions are clear add 1½ cups milk, herbs, Worcestershire, and cayenne and bring to a boil. In a small bowl whisk the flour with last ½ cup of the milk until lumpless and add to the pot. Cover and reduce to low simmer for 15 minutes. Then add turkey and corn. Simmer 10 minutes more. Salt and pepper to taste. 6 servings give or take.

Janowski's Cabbage Soup

Hearty and wholesome

2 cups vegetable stock

2 medium potatoes - peeled and cut in chunks

¼ pound cooked smoked deli ham - chopped or diced

¼ cabbage - cored and shredded

salt and pepper to taste

3 tablespoons minced fresh parsley

1 clove garlic - mashed or pressed

¼ onion - minced

1 carrot - peeled and shredded

1 rib celery - shredded

1 cup navy beans - cooked or canned

1 bay leaf - you can't go wrong with a bay leaf

Place stock and potatoes in large soup pot and bring to boil. Add the cabbage and remaining ingredients (with the exception of the navy beans and meat), cover and simmer until potatoes are tender - about 20 minutes. Add navy beans and meat and continue simmering 10 minutes more. Adjust seasoning. Serve with toasted French bread slices, and don't eat the bay leaf. Serves 3 or 4.

Around 1910, when my uncles began marketing vegetables locally and state-wide, their best sellers were cabbage, celery, and parsnips.

Every July we supply the St. Nicholas Ukranian Catholic Church of Elmira Heights with *hundreds* of heads of cabbage for their church festival.

Backside view of our two barns, dated March 1959.

Triple C Chowder
Corn, Carrot, Chicken (or Crab)
Delicious and easy to prepare

3 tablespoons butter or margarine
1 rib celery - minced
1 carrot - cut thinly
½ cup onion - minced
3 tablespoons flour dissolved in a little water
¼ teaspoon dried dill optional - added right before serving
2 cups chicken broth
2 cups milk
2 cups fresh corn kernels (I puree one cup but you can leave them whole)
2 cups chicken - cooked and cut into small pieces or 1 can crabmeat
Salt and freshly ground pepper to taste

In a large saucepan, melt the butter and add the celery and onion. Sauté for 5-8 minutes over medium-low heat, or until vegetables are softened. In a small bowl, whisk the flour with about 3 tablespoons of water until smooth and set aside. Add the chicken broth and milk to pot. Stir well. Reduce heat and simmer, covered for 20 minutes. Add the corn, chicken or crab. Bring back to a boil and season to taste. You can thicken the soup at this point with the flour/water mixture. If desired add the dill now. Reduce and simmer 5 more minutes. 6 servings.

25

Potato and Green Onion Soup
Perfect for a nice light lunch

1 bunch green onions - finely chopped (green part too)

1 rib celery - finely chopped

3 big potatoes - cut in chunks

5 cups milk

2 tablespoons flour dissolved in 2 tablespoons water

Olive oil

Vegetable or chicken bouillon powder to season 4 cups of liquid

Tabasco to taste

salt and pepper

Fresh chives - chopped

Boil and mash potatoes - can be chunky if you like. I do! In pan, sauté celery in a little olive oil and water about 10 minutes. Add green onions and sauté one more minute. Remove from heat.

In big pot, combine potatoes, milk, celery, onions, bouillon and flour / water. Bring to boiling, adjust with salt and pepper, and Tabasco, and it's ready to serve - sprinkle chives over soup.

For any recipe in this book that calls for milk you really can use whatever you like - whole, skim, soy, cream, half & half, or fat-free half & half. Any recipe that calls for mayonnaise or sour cream you may easily substitute low-fat, no- fat, yogurt, or soy versions. We do like Olivio margarine for a buttery flavor with no trans fats.

Vegetables du Jour Soup

Choose the vegetables you like

3 tablespoons olive oil
½ onion - chopped
1 rib celery - chopped
1 carrot - sliced
1 potato - diced
6 cups chicken broth
salt and pepper to taste
1 teaspoon fresh or dried parsley
3 cups of your choice of diced vegetables (cauliflower, green beans, cabbage, zucchini, corn, broccoli, spinach, green or red peppers, eggplant)
Optional: 1 cup cooked diced meat (chicken, turkey, beef, ground beef)

In large pot, heat oil. Add onion, celery, potato and stir. Add chicken broth, bring to a boil, then cover and simmer 20 minutes. Add vegetables and seasonings, bring to a boil, add cooked meat, then simmer 10 minutes or until vegetables are tender.

In the early 1960s when I was little, I remember "making the daily rounds" with my grandparents or my father - when we would deliver vegetables to many of the neighborhood groceries in Elmira. The ones I can recall are the Mohawk, Ostrander's, Elias's, and Snyder's. What I remember most is that as a little blonde kid, every store owner gave me something - ice cream, popsicles, Coca-Cola, slices of cheddar cheese or meat, and hard candy. This happened *every* day. My mom never knew why I wasn't hungry at home. In the middle 1960s, my father started delivering to food brokers like Flickinger's, Empire Foods, and several larger supermarkets. These daily trips took longer because the loads were much bigger. My dad took us for ice cream cones at Big Nine on Grand Central Avenue.

CHEMUNG

N

Jno. Donahue

L. Robinson

C. Callahan

Mrs. Murray

Samuels & Strauss

M! Reedy

T. Flannery

A. Burchell

L. Murphy

Mrs. Watkins

J.ⁿ Brand

Mrs. Dempsey

A. Burchell

C. Callahan

Davis Heirs

M. Murray

Jas. Dick

C. Callahan

M. Callahans Hrs.

Davis Hrs

D. Daley

F. Geneski

H! Murray

J.ⁿ Donahue

Rob! Bell

W.ᵐ Maloney

Mrs. Young

G. Hinch

Mrs. Watkins

F. Geneski

C. Connolly

Dd. Robinson

ROBINSON ST.

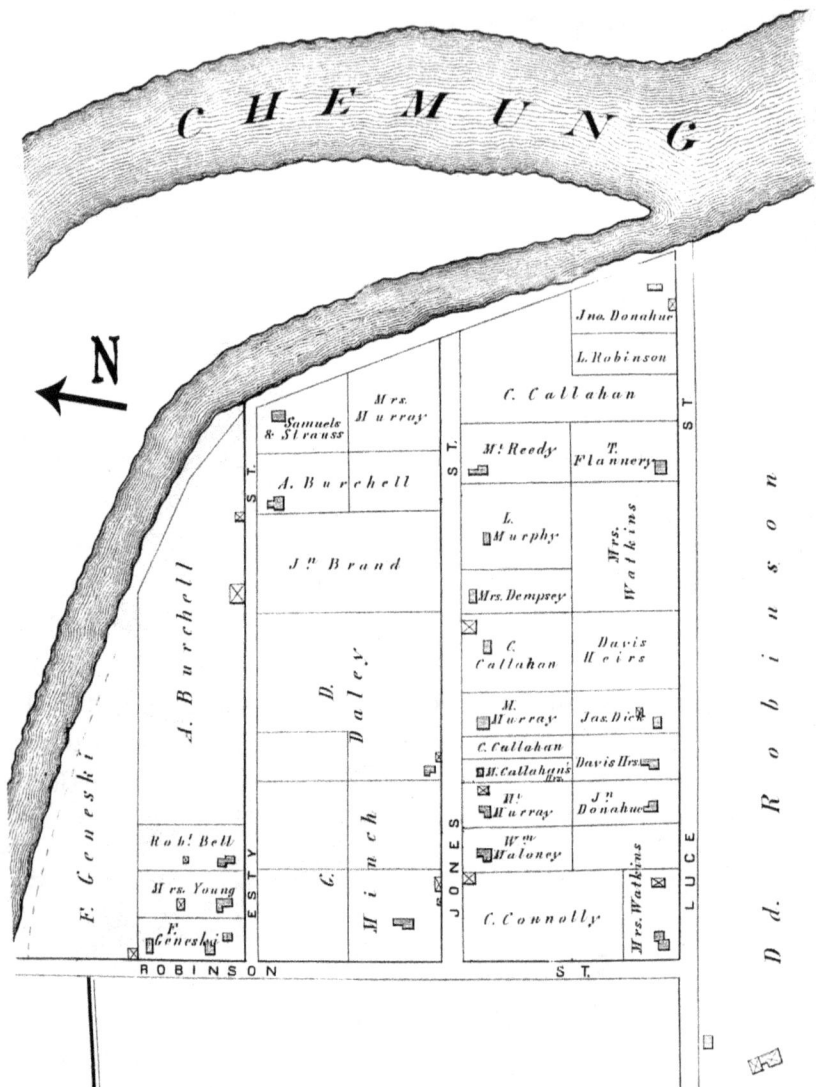

The first parcel of our farm is on the bottom left - marked F. Geneski - I told you ear-
lier about the misspellings. Note the branch of the Chemung River that once went
through our property. Our levee (probably the dotted line on our property above)
was built to keep the river off our vegetables. Our woods is now where the river
used to be. This part of the river was cut off with the building of the state's (several)
levees through Elmira beginning around the time of the 1889 flood. It was a pond
for many years before it dried up. There are several photos of our levee in this book.
This map was dated 1876. On opposite page is a current aerial photo of our farm.

The white lines denote our farm in 2008. Note that the swath of trees through the middle is our woods and follows the path of the branch of the river in the map on the opposite page.

Hearty Pureed Vegetable Soup

Pick your favorites!

2 tablespoons olive oil

½ onion - diced

1 rib celery - diced

3 cups chicken or vegetable broth

3 cups of vegetables (your choice of cauliflower, kale, broccoli, spinach, mushrooms, red peppers, carrots, potatoes)

1 tablespoon fresh or dried parsley

2 pinches of your favorite herbs or spices (such as basil, curry, thyme, ginger, white pepper, or cayenne pepper)

2 cups milk

1 green onion - sliced for garnish

Tabasco, and salt and pepper to taste

Heat oil in big pot. Sauté the onion and celery. Add chicken broth, seasonings, and vegetables, bring to a boil, cover and simmer 20 minutes. Then with a hand blender, purée the vegetables in the soup. Add milk or cream to desired consistency. Season to taste. Reheat. Serve in bowls with green onion as garnish.

Basil Butter
This makes a lot

½ cup fresh basil leaves - stemmed

8 tablespoons (one stick) salted butter or margarine - softened

Freshly ground pepper to taste

Using kitchen shears, finely snip basil leaves and add to softened butter. Mix well and season to taste. Reshape butter in small bowl or fancy mold and chill. Unmold if desired. Basil butter is excellent on grilled lamb chops, steak, chicken or steamed vegetables.

We love basil. I have a Ronco™ food dehydrator that I love dearly. Annually I dry basil, parsley, thyme, oregano, dill, catnip, celery, cilantro, and jalapeño peppers (yes, but I do it outdoors) with great success.

Vegetables in our farm stand, 2005.

Warm or Cold Basil Cream Sauce
A nice sauce or dip for fresh vegetables

¼ cup dry white wine

1 tablespoon Dijon or Creole mustard

½ cup fresh basil leaves - chopped

1 or 2 cloves garlic - minced or pressed

¼ cup olive oil

1 cup sour cream

½ cup plain yogurt (can be non-fat)

3 tablespoons fresh parsley - minced

Tony's Creole Seasoning or salt and freshly ground pepper to taste

Combine wine, mustard, basil and garlic in a hand blender container. Add oil, sour cream, yogurt and parsley and process with hand blender until smooth. Season to taste with salt and pepper. Can be served warm or cold. Makes about 3 cups.

Andalouse Sauce

Oh my gosh this is good. Great on French fries instead of ketchup, or a secret sauce on hamburgers, vegetables or fish, also works as a dip for vegetables.

1 cup mayonnaise
2 tablespoons tomato paste
2 tablespoons - onion - finely chopped (or puréed)
1 tablespoon red pepper – finely chopped (or puréed)
1 tablespoon green pepper -– finely chopped (or puréed)
1 tablespoon fresh lemon or lime juice - I like lime
¼ teaspoon salt
1 good pinch of cilantro
dash of Tabasco

Stir together and chill. Needs an hour for the flavors to *mélange* together. Serve at room temperature.

Dogs and kittens do play nice together. From left to right: great-Uncle Fritz, cousin Mildred, and great-Aunt Margaret holding kittens. The dog on the right is Rex - he is in many family photos - never on a tractor, though. Circa 1915.

Chopping wood to keep the barns and greenhouse warm circa 1925. We still chop wood to keep our main barn warm. Our greenhouse is still used although not kept warm year round anymore. Below, 2005.

SALAD DAYS

"Janowski's Best" our World War II crew, circa 1946, included cousin Janice (Beaty) an unknown girl, Onalee Hartman Graves, and cousin Doris (Houghtalen). My father says that during the war we employed many high school girls. Janice, above left, edited a weekly Janowski Gardens newspaper for employees for 3 years.

A farm was always a good place to work during rough times. During the Depression we employed around 40 employees. The wholesale vegetable business was doing well - big trucks came and loaded our vegetables and took them to sell in Rochester and Pennsylvania.

My father in 2006.

Bob's Baby Mixed Greens Salad and Dressing
We love baby mixed greens

4 cups baby mixed greens
1 cup cherry tomatoes
4 slices red onion
3 tablespoon chopped Louisiana pecans
¼ cup crumbly cheese - sometimes you can find a nice no-fat feta

Toss together.

Mixed Greens Salad Dressing

2 tablespoons red wine or raspberry vinegar
¼ cup olive oil
½ teaspoon chopped oregano
Salt and pepper to taste

Mix these ingredients. Toss with greens.

Mixed Baby Greens with Tarragon Vinaigrette

Hints of honey and mustard

Mixed Greens are our best selling product!

6 cups of greens
2 tablespoons white wine or apple cider vinegar
1 good pinch tarragon leaves - minced or dry
2 tablespoons balsamic vinegar
2 teaspoons Dijon or Creole mustard
2 teaspoons honey
salt and pepper to taste
½ cup olive oil

Wash greens and spin or pat dry. Whisk vinegars, tarragon, mustard, honey, salt and pepper in a small bowl. Slowly add in the oil. Toss with greens just before serving.

Our woods are the nicest place in the whole world. Photo, 2005.

I have a feeling that cabbage is a genetic thing. From left to right: great Uncle Gus, cousin Mildred, great Uncle Fritz, and great Uncle Charlie Schiller, and unknown man circa 1914.

Janowski's Southside Cole Slaw
I'm in a Southside state of mind

Half a cabbage - coarsely shredded
1 or 2 green onions (scallions) sliced
2 tablespoons apple cider or red wine vinegar
¾ cup mayonnaise (or plain yogurt)
½ teaspoon fresh ground pepper
½ teaspoon dill
1 tablespoon fresh parsley
2 teaspoons honey
½ teaspoon salt
2 teaspoons raw or brown sugar
1 teaspoon Dijon or Creole mustard
A couple of shots of McIlhenny's Tabasco to taste.
Optional: ¼ Granny Smith apple shredded (if you use apple - mix it with the vinegar from above in a small bowl so it doesn't oxidize).

Place cabbage in large bowl. Add onion to cabbage. Mix vinegar, mayonnaise, honey, mustard, Tabasco, and apple together. Set aside. Just before serving add dressing to chopped cabbage. Then season with salt, pepper, and dill to taste.

A Slaw of Many Colors

This is very impressive

½ cabbage - shredded
1 carrot - shredded
4 radishes - shredded, be careful - this is hard to do
½ red pepper - shredded
½ apple - shredded
Fresh parsley to taste
2 teaspoons onion - minced
¼ teaspoon dill

Sauce
¾ cup mayonnaise
2 tablespoons apple cider vinegar
1 teaspoon lime juice
1 teaspoon raw or brown sugar

Combine sauce ingredients in a small bowl. Mix salad ingredients in a bigger bowl. Mix sauce and salad.

Denny's Perfect Balsamic Vinaigrette Dressing

Yes, it is perfect

¼ cup olive oil
2 tablespoons Balsamic vinegar
½ teaspoon dry mustard powder
½ teaspoon coarsely ground pepper
¼ teaspoon garlic powder
2 good shakes Tabasco
½ teaspoon dry oregano
Optional: 1 pinch of tarragon, basil, cilantro, or dried celery. Mix and match what you like.

Mix together. Let sit a few minutes. Pour over salad. Makes enough for 2.

Above, out surveying the property, circa 1910. This road was called the Brand Flat Road, along the Chemung River (it went around the edge of our property) - it's where the levee is today. Looking east toward Jerusalem Hill. Don't know who the people are.

Left, great-Aunt Margaret on the left, and cousin Mildred on right. Margaret was the baby of the family and lived to the age of 100. Photo circa 1915.

Collard Greens Cole Slaw

This is definitely a recipe that I would think of

Five leaves of collard greens – washed and ribs removed- ribs are too tough for raw eating!

Two carrots shredded

2 tablespoons apple cider vinegar, or champagne vinegar

½ cup mayonnaise

½ tablespoon raw sugar

White or black pepper to taste

Stack collard leaves and fold over. With a sharp knife – cut very thin shreds about 1/8". In a small mixing bowl, mix the vinegar, mayonnaise, sugar, and pepper. In larger bowl, mix shredded greens and shredded carrots, and dressing. Enjoy.

Grampa plowing along Robinson Street (before the houses were built). Note Riverside School in the right background, circa 1945.

Arugula Farm Salad with Lime Ginger Dressing
Zesty and citrus-y

1½ cups arugula (you can substitute any other salad greens)

1½ cups dark red lettuce

½ cup crumbly cheese – Bleu, Feta – or even a nice fat-free Feta

½ Vidalia onion sliced

¼ cup Louisiana pecans – or find the best you can

Toss these ingredients.

Lime Ginger Salad Dressing

¼ cup olive oil

2 tablespoons fresh lime juice

½ teaspoon grated ginger

salt and pepper to taste

Mix dressing ingredients. Pour over salad and toss.

Growing what they sell makes Janowski's No. 1

Gardens wins as best fruit, vegetable stand

By DEBORAH MORGAN
Star-Gazette

Fruit and vegetable stands may pop up like summer squash along the roadsides every year, but come May 1, everyone knows Janowski Gardens opens its door for the some of the plumpest produce pickin's around.

The family-owned and operated market won the best fruit and vegetable stand category in the Star-Gazette's *What's Hot* contest — and they won with 82 percent of the vote. They are open from 9 a.m. to 7 p.m. seven days a week.

"We're old-fashioned, like things used to be," said Robert Janowski, who with his wife, Hilda, and his brother, Paul, own the market located at 517 Esty St. on Elmira's Southside.

They have 15 acres of farmland that curls around the back of Robinson street toward Brand Park. Everything they sell comes from that land.

"Our motto is, 'We grow what we sell,'" said Janowski. "When we run out of something, we go pick some more. We don't have any refrigeration, so what you see is fresh picked."

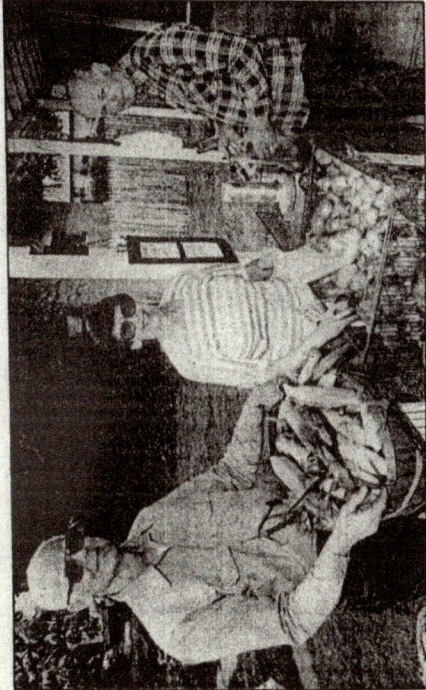

FRUITS AND VEGETABLES: Robert Janowski (left), his wife, Hilda, and brother, Paul, offer fresh produce at their stand on Esty Street, Elmira.

JEFF RICHARDS/Star-Gazette

You'll find bushel baskets and wire carts full of onions, corn, melons, lettuce, squash, tomatoes and other veggies and fruits at their open-air market located behind their home. A sign on the road directs you to the driveway — a sleeping calico cat yawns as you pull in. Hilda Janowski's big smile tells you you're at the right place.

"It's quiet here, cooler, peaceful," said Robert Janowski, whose parents and uncles ran the gardens as a wholesale produce operation until he and his brother Paul took it over in 1965.

During the summer, they usually have a couple of workers help out in the fields. This year, the three have been on their own. "They said it was too hot to work and quit," said Hilda Janowski. "So we've been doing it all."

Times are tough — because of the drought. They said at this time of the year they usually have so many bushel baskets of produce you can barely make a path through the open-air mar- ket. Today, there are half full baskets of melons and no winter squash at all. Still, the tomatoes are red and firm, and there's lots of onions and potatoes and other Elmira-grown goodies.

"People like our corn," said Hilda Janowski. "A lot of people who have lived here come back to visit and make it a point to buy our corn. They take it home with them all over the country."

Although the drought has slashed stock, and therefore this year's profits, the Janowskis aren't new to tough times. On the wall of the market are lines in black paint marking the height of flood waters during the 1946 and 1972 floods.

"This is probably the worst year outside of those two years," said Robert Janowski, who joined his parents and uncles operation in 1949. "They were complete disasters — this wasn't quite that bad — it just wasn't good!"

His wife added, "We're going to get by."

During the off-season, the Janowskis plan the next year's crop. The greenhouse planting begins in February. If you like to travel, Janowski said owning a market like this isn't for you.

"If you want to stay put, it's alright — especially if you like to work seven days a week, 12 hours a day," he chuckled.

> **Other people retire to grow a garden. What do I have to retire for?**
> Robert Janowski

But if you're one of the folks who walks across the block or drives in twice a week from Steuben County to snap up squash or cabbage or lettuce don't despair — Janowski's is here to stay.

Robert Janowski smiled: "Other people retire to grow a garden. What do I have to retire for?"

Reprinted with permission of the Elmira *Star-Gazette*.

Vegetables

My father and Uncle Paul planting tomatoes, May 20, 1998. Photo by Nancy Parker.

Something Good Zucchini

Something good does come from zucchini

1 zucchini - cut in ½ inch slices

½ Spanish onion - sliced

7 baby portobella or brown mushrooms - sliced

¼ cup water

1 teaspoon minced garlic

Salt and pepper to taste (or Tony's - a Creole seasoning)

¼ cup plain bread crumbs

Balsamic vinegar

4 tablespoons olive oil

In large frying pan, sauté onions and garlic in olive oil. Add zucchini and mushrooms, water, salt and pepper, cover and cook gently for about 15 minutes. Add several dashes of balsamic vinegar. Cook two minutes then add enough bread crumbs to thicken juices slightly. Cook two minutes longer and serve immediately.

Denny and I both regularly suffer from hypoglycemia so we try to eat healthy snacks in-between meals to keep our blood sugar levels steady. In the mornings we like Trail Mix bars, in the afternoons cheese and whole wheat crackers.

Buckhorn Beans

Sloooow cooked Southern green beans. Heaven in your mouth!

Denny and I have a favorite restaurant (the Buckhorn Café) in Lottie, Louisiana on Interstate 190 where the food and service are great. We go there as often as possible. This is the closest I can come to their green beans.

4 slices of bacon - diced

½ onion - diced

salt and pepper to taste

1 pound green beans (cut 1" pieces, ends snipped)

2 cups water

In big pot slightly fry the bacon - not too brown - you want the bacon to be a little lively. Add beans and stir. Add rest of ingredients and water. Bring to boil, then cover and reduce to simmer. Simmer slooowly for 50 minutes. Check every once in a while and add water if necessary (bring back to a boil, then simmer). Then remove lid, increase heat to moderate simmer for 10 more minutes. Mmm good.

My Favorite Spinach Sandwich

2 slices bread

mayonnaise

spinach

Spread mayonnaise on bread. Put on some spinach. Put bread on top. Enjoy.

Same location different year - top circa 1910, bottom circa 2005. Both, from the Chemung River levee looking northwest toward downtown Elmira. Top photo you can see the smokestacks from the Riverside power plant on East Water Street.

Picking potatoes in 2005. From left to right: my father Robert, Denny Smith, and Uncle Paul. In bottom photo, my father from a potato's eye view.

Baked Potatoes with Guacamole Sauce

Sour cream with a green zesty twist

4 baked potatoes

1 avocado – cut in four sections

½ cup sour cream or plain yogurt

½ teaspoon dry cilantro or 1 teaspoon fresh chopped cilantro

1 tablespoon of lime juice

pepper to taste

McIlhenny's Tabasco to taste

Cut avocado into four sections. Take one section and put in mixing bowl, and wrap the remaining 3 quarters in freezer wrap and freeze for later use. Yes, the pieces freeze well.

Mash avocado piece in bowl with sour cream and all other ingredients.

Top baked potatoes with sauce. Perfect. Sauce is also good as a dip.

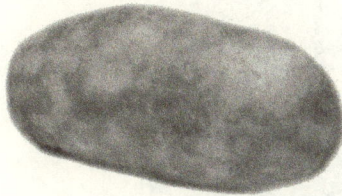

A nice looking potato.

Hot German Potato Salad

You can't go wrong with potato salad

3 medium potatoes - hot, cooked and sliced into ¼" slices
4 slices bacon - diced
½ onion - chopped

Sauce
½ cup white or apple cider vinegar
3 tablespoons water
1 tablespoon brown sugar
salt and black pepper to taste

In pan, fry bacon and onion - when brown enough for you add sauce ingredients and heat to boiling. Pour over hot potatoes and serve. Enough for 3 or 4 servings.

How hot is it? The official farm thermometer on the barn wall, 2006.

Fresh tilled ground waiting for something to be planted in it, 2006

Special Corn Bread

Breakfast, Lunch or Dinner

1 package of Jiffy™ cornbread mix

2/3 cup milk

2 slices jalapeño pepper - then minced

4 teaspoons cooked corn kernels - mashed or pureed

I have found there is a secret to preparing the cornbread mix - the package says 1/3 cup milk **but use 2/3 cup milk.** It takes a little longer to bake but is much moister and much better. Prepare mix with the extra milk, add jalapeños and corn. Bake until done.

Farmer Denny's Southern and Northern Kale

A one-cup serving of kale has the highest carotenoids of ALL vegetables.

Here are 2 versions of the same recipe - one for Southerners and one for Northerners. Farmer Denny prefers the Southern version - but you can decide for yourself. Makes 2 large side dishes or 4 small. All we are saying is, "Give Kale a Chance."

Farmer Denny's Southern Kale

1 bunch kale greens - cut off stems and ribs
1 cup chicken or vegetable broth
1 cup water
1 piece of diced meat (optional) - such as one good slice of cooked ham, one small link of cooked andouille or chorizo sausage, one cooked pork chop, etc, or you can leave as vegetarian
McIlhenny's Tabasco

Wash and stack greens on top of each other. With knife cut across greens making one-inch strips. Stacking them speeds up the process as you are cutting through all leaves at once. In large pot add stock, water, and greens. Bring to boil, add meat if desired, then cover and reduce to gentle simmer. It needs to simmer about 2 and a half hours to achieve perfection, but it will be well worth it and your house will smell wonderful. Please stir pot every half-hour and add more water if necessary. Add as much Tabasco you like. Farmer Denny likes kale greens with a side of Sylvia's™ black-eyed peas. Enjoy.

Next time, after you decide that you really do like kale, you can double or triple this recipe and experiment with other meats. It also freezes well - just portion it into freezer bags.

Farmer Denny's Northern Kale

Crunchy and lively

1 bunch kale greens - cut off stems and ribs

½ cup chicken or vegetable stock

Olive oil

1 piece of diced meat (optional) - such as one slice of cooked ham, one small link of cooked andouille or chorizo sausage, one cooked pork chop, etc, or you can leave as vegetarian

Vegetable bouillon powder or salt and pepper to taste

McIlhenny's Tabasco to taste

Wash and stack greens on top of each other. With knife cut across greens making one-inch strips. Stacking them speeds up the process as you are cutting through all leaves at once. In large saute pan add a little olive oil, stock, Tabasco, seasonings, and greens. Saute until desired tenderness - maybe 5 - 10 minutes, add a little water if needed, and meat. Enjoy.

Eat more kale.

Creole Vegetable Jambalaya

Goodbye Joe, me gotta go...

1 cup red or yellow onions - diced

1 cup bell peppers - diced

1 cup celery - diced

½ cup okra - sliced - come on, you won't even notice

½ cup corn

1 cup yellow squash - diced

1 cup zucchini - diced

1 tablespoon minced garlic

3 cups chopped tomatoes – canned is fine (be sure to drain)

Salt and freshly ground black pepper, to taste

½ to 1 teaspoon cayenne pepper, to taste (optional)

Tony's Creole seasoning or salt and pepper to taste

½ teaspoon dried thyme

2 bay leaves

4 cups uncooked long grain rice

1 cup tomato sauce

8 cups vegetable stock

1 cup chopped green onions

Olive oil

Heat 3 tablespoons olive oil in a large heavy pot over medium heat. Add the squash, and zucchini, and sauté until they're tender, 5 minutes or so. Put squash in bowl and set aside. Heat 3 more tablespoons olive oil and sauté the onions, bell peppers, okra, and garlic until tender, about 5 minutes. Add the tomatoes. Add seasonings. Add the bay leaves and rice and stir. Add the tomato sauce. Add the vegetable stock, stir, bring to a boil, Cover and reduce to simmer. Cook for 30 to 35 minutes, or until the rice is tender and the liquid has been absorbed. Do not stir the jambalaya while it's cooking. When the rice is done, add the squash, stir, remove from heat and let stand for 2-3 minutes. Add the green onions and mix thoroughly. Don't eat the bay leaves.

Yield: 12 servings

Here is my dad, fresh from the Army, with our greenhouse. Just to the right of him is the tobacco barn along Liberty Street. Photo dated March 1959.

Stuffed Peppers

Not mushy, soupy, goopy, gray, or anything like you remember - I would never do that to a pepper

"The best Spanish rice I've ever had." Denny Smith

2 big green peppers

1 cup uncooked rice

2 cups vegetable stock

1 pinch oregano

½ teaspoon cumin

½ teaspoon chili powder

1 clove garlic - minced or garlic powder to taste

1 cup (8 oz.) your favorite salsa

ground beef (about one hamburger's worth)

salt and pepper to taste

Preheat oven to 350°. In a big pot, brown the meat. In same pot, add rice, water, spices, and vegetable broth. Bring to a boil, then cover and reduce heat to low. Cook until water is absorbed about 20 minutes.

When rice is done, remove from heat and add salsa. Stir to blend. Grease small casserole dish, fill with rice, and bake partially covered about 20 minutes to allow rice to absorb the salsa.

While rice is baking, cut the peppers in half the long way - like the picture - and cut out seeds and stem. In pan, heat olive oil and a little water and sauté peppers several minutes on each side - just long enough to get them slightly soft and hot. Remove and arrange on plate inside up. Fill each half with rice and meat. Enjoy.

Diane's Unstuffed Cabbage Casserole

No where near as good as St. Nicholas Ukranian Church cabbage rolls, but still pretty good

½ cabbage - cored and cut in half (again, so 2 quarter chunks)

ground beef - about 2 hamburger's worth - browned

2 cups beef, chicken or vegetable broth

caraway seeds to taste

2 cups cooked rice - white or wild or combination

½ onion - diced

1 clove of garlic - diced

1 tablespoon dried or fresh chopped parsley

paprika to taste - I like the hot Hungarian kind

3 tablespoons tomato sauce

salt and pepper to taste

In a big pot, heat water and boil the cabbage uncovered about 20 minutes until tender. (In the beginning poke it every few minutes to get the leaves apart.) Preheat oven to 400°. In small pan, sauté onions and garlic. When cabbage is tender, remove from heat and drain. In big baking dish, layer cabbage on bottom, sprinkle on the garlic, onions, caraway seeds, and parsley. Season to taste on each level. Then meat. Then rice. Mix the paprika and tomato sauce into the broth and pour broth over all. Bake partially covered for 30 minutes.

Janowski Corned Beef and Cabbage

We might be German, but we like it too!

½ medium cabbage
½ pound sliced deli corned beef
3 whole cloves
1 teaspoon brown sugar
1 bay leaf
¼ teaspoon dried basil
2 cups chicken broth
2 tablespoons minced onion
1 teaspoon minced or dried parlsey

Cut the half cabbage in half (again, 2 quarter wedges) put in large pot. Add chicken broth and then add extra water to pot to bring liquid level to about 2 inches of water. Add rest of ingredients except corned beef. Bring to boil, (in the beginning poke cabbage every few minutes to get the leaves apart) then simmer covered at least a half hour up to an hour depending on how tender you like your cabbage - I like mine a little lively. Add corned beef and simmer 5 more minutes. Serve, and don't eat the bay leaf or the cloves.

Edamame - Our Newest Vegetable (ed-a-ma-may)

Japanese Soy Beans

Rinse fresh edamame pods. Put pods into briskly boiling water. Cook to second boil 2-5 minutes or until tender. At this stage, you will normally notice some pods opening up. Do not overcook. Drain water, let cool, sprinkle with salt and serve.

Eating Directions:
Take soybean pod by the stem, place between teeth, strip soybeans from the pod with your teeth and discard empty pods.

Cabbage, cabbage as far as the eye can see, circa 1919. From left to right cousins Eleanor and Mildred, and Uncle Fritz. Note the tobacco barn in the back - we had one tobacco barn - this one isn't it. My father says we owned all the land in this photo around this barn - but not the barn. Our farm was once owned by John Brand who had a tobacco plantation (over 600 acres on the Southside). I remember this barn from early childhood. It was along Liberty Street. It was torn down around 1963.

Below, this *is* our tobacco barn. You can see the barn behind my father on his sled! Circa 1932. We never grew tobacco but the barns came in handy for storage.

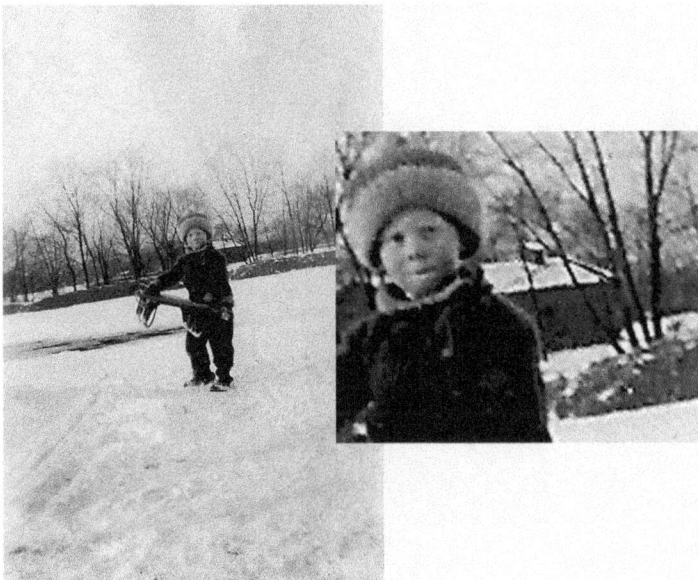

Secret Janowski Sauerkraut

This recipe was used for many generations of sauerkraut suppers at the old German Church (the First United Church of Christ) on Madison Avenue. This should keep you busy:

40 pounds grated cabbage
½ pound kosher salt

In big crock, pack cabbage with salt on top. Cover with a clean cloth or plate or any board except pine. When fermentation begins, remove scum daily and change cloth daily. Best sauerkraut is made at temperatures 60 degrees or lower for at least one month. When fermentation has stopped, seal with a layer of paraffin over surface.

*The secret to my sauerkraut is Silver Floss™ in the bag.

German Fried Potatoes
Good for breakfast, lunch or dinner

2 cold boiled potatoes - sliced
salt and pepper to taste
1 tablespoon butter
paprika to taste
olive oil

In frying pan, sauté potatoes until golden brown. Season with salt and pepper and paprika.

Love Mushrooms

Make these for someone you love! A private display of affection.

8 baby portabello mushrooms

¼ cup cheese (any kind soft or shredded cheese)

Dollop of sour cream or 3 tablespoons milk or cream

small quantity of bread crumbs

pinch parsley

¼ teaspoon minced garlic

pinch of your favorite spice

dash Worcestershire sauce

salt and pepper to taste

Red or white wine

Olive oil

Parmesan cheese

Preheat oven to 350°. Wash mushrooms and twist stem out of cap. Chop 4 of the stems as finely as you can. In mixing bowl, add chopped stems, sour cream or cream, Worcestershire, garlic, parsley, salt and pepper. Add some bread crumbs - just enough to make it a little stiff. In baking dish, add a little olive oil to bottom and swish around. Fill mushroom caps with about a tablespoon of the mixture and arrange in baking dish. Add a little wine to the bottom of the baking dish - about 4 or 5 tablespoons. Sprinkle parmesan cheese or more bread crumbs over tops of mushrooms and bake uncovered in oven about 10 - 15 minutes.

Corn on the Cob

We grow the hybrid "Butter & Sugar" corn that produces ears of yellow and white kernels. B&S has been a longtime mainstay of roadside stands and farmers' markets in the Northeast.

The sugar level in corn immediately after picking begins its gradual conversion to starch that, in turn, lessens the corn's natural sweetness. Look for ears with bright green, snugly fitting husks and golden brown silk. The kernels should be plump and milky and come all the way to the ear's tip; the rows should be tightly spaced.

Fresh corn should be cooked and served the day it's purchased, but it can be refrigerated up to a day. But why wait?

Eat now – get more tomorrow. Strip off the husks and silk just before cooking.

The way we cook it is to get a big pot of water boiling on the stove and put the corn in for 3 minutes – we like them crunchy and lively. Rearrange them in the water every minute to ensure equal cooking. Then we serve the corn with margarine and Tony's (our favorite seasoning from Opelousas, Louisiana www.tonychachere.com) or salt and pepper.

Corn Chowder
Sort of a Maque Choux soup

2 tablespoons butter or margarine

3 tablespoons flour dissolved in 6 tablespoons water

1 cup vegetable stock

2 cups milk

1 slice of onion - minced

¼ cup red peppers - chopped

½ cup corn (one ear)

salt and pepper to taste

dash of cayenne pepper

olive oil

salt and pepper to taste

Sauté onion, corn, and red peppers in pot with a little olive oil. Add butter and add flour/water mixture, stock and milk and bring to boil, then simmer uncovered 10 minutes. Season to taste.

My favorite cookbooks are:

Mandy's Favorite Louisiana Recipes
River Road Recipes (Baton Rouge Junior League)
Paul Prudhomme's Louisiana Kitchen

Pasta

Here is my mom, Hildegard, behind the counter in our vegetable stand behind our house, circa 1995.

Asparagus or Broccoli Lemon Pasta
Very zesty with a bright lemon flavor

½ pound asparagus or broccoli cut into 1" pieces

½ pound bow-tie pasta

½ red pepper - diced

3 tablespoons butter

1½ cups milk

½ tablespoon freshly grated lemon zest

2 tablespoons fresh lemon juice

salt and pepper to taste

½ teaspoon minced garlic

Vegetable or chicken bouillon powder - (enough to season 1 ½ cups liquid)

1 tablespoon cornstarch mixed with 2 tablespoons cold water in small bowl

Accompaniment: Freshly grated Parmesan or Asiago cheese

Steam asparagus or broccoli until it is tender (anywhere from 2 to 10 minutes - I like mine still crunchy). Immediately transfer to colander and rinse with cold water. Place on paper towels to drain. Cook pasta until *al dente*, and drain. In pot, heat butter and sauté red peppers and garlic for several minutes then add milk, bouillon, seasonings, and cornstarch mixture and heat until boiling, stir in lemon zest, lemon juice, and pepper. When sauce thickens add cooked pasta and asparagus or broccoli and heat about 1 minute). Serve with grated Parmesan or Asiago cheese.

For any recipe in this book that calls for milk you really can use whatever you like - whole, skim, soy, cream, half & half, or fat-free half & half. Any recipe that calls for butter you may easily substitute margarine. We prefer no trans fat margarine like Olivio.

Pasta with Fresh Tomato and Mozzarella
A cool pasta salad for hot summer days

4 tablespoons olive oil

1 small onion - diced

1 clove garlic - pressed or minced

3 medium tomatoes - seeded and chopped

¼ pound mozzarella (or fat-free mozzarella) - shredded

½ cup basil leaves - stemmed and chopped

Red pepper flakes to taste - adds some zip

Freshly ground pepper to taste

1 tablespoon balsamic vinegar

Freshly grated Parmesan (can be fat-free)

½ pound cooked cold pasta - your choice

salt and pepper to taste

In small skillet, heat olive oil. Add onion and garlic and cook over low heat. Remove from heat. In large bowl, combine sautéed onion/garlic, with tomatoes, mozzarella, chopped basil, pepper flakes, oregano, salt and pepper, and balsamic vinegar. Mix with pasta, adjust seasoning and serve at room temperature with freshly grated parmesan cheese. Serves 2 to 4.

Some photos inside our vegetable stand - baskets of tomatoes above, and a good year for pumpkins below, circa 2004.

Linguine with Basil Cream and Tomatoes
A fresh alternative to red sauce

4 tablespoons olive oil

1 clove garlic - minced

1 medium tomato or 12 cherry tomatoes - chopped

2 cups milk or cream

¼ cup basil leaves - stemmed and chopped

2 tablespoons cornstarch mixed with 4 tablespoons cold water in small bowl

Vegetable bouillon powder or salt and pepper to taste

½ pound linguine (dry weight) cooked and drained

grated Parmesan or Asiago cheese

In large skillet, heat olive oil over low heat. Add garlic and tomatoes. Sauté until tomatoes begin to soften. Add milk or cream, and cornstarch/water and cook until slightly thickened (about 5 minutes). Season with bouillon or salt and pepper, add chopped basil leaves, and toss with hot pasta. Top with parmesan cheese. Serves 2 or 3 hungry people.

Basil is the herb that I use the most.

Cheese and Eggs

Our 1968 International Harvester Cub Hi Boy - still going strong in 2008. We also have a new New Holland TT-A Series tractor for doing the big tough stuff.

"As God is my witness I'll never be hungry again." Denny Smith in a *Gone With the Wind* moment. Actually, we were uncovering the young peppers after a near freeze experience. Photo circa 2001 before the highway crews cut the trees on the hill in the background.

Jalapeño Quiche

Really hot – Helps if you have a cast iron stomach!

1 pie shell - ready to bake
3 eggs (or equivalent Egg Beaters™)
1 cup milk or cream
1 cup shredded cheese – gruyere, fontina, cheddar or combination
½ cup bread crumbs
4 jalapeños - sliced and seeded
1 teaspoon chili powder
¼ teaspoon cumin
1 teaspoon dried parsley or 2 tablespoons fresh
1½ teaspoons butter or margarine
Salt and pepper to taste

Preheat oven to 375 °. In pie shell, arrange jalapeños on the bottom. In mixing bowl, beat eggs and other ingredients. Pour over peppers and bake uncovered 30 - 45 minutes until bubbly and top is browned, and when inserted toothpick comes out clean.

Toad in a Hole

No toads are harmed in the preparation of this recipe!
Good for breakfast or a light meal

3 small link breakfast sausages or soy sausages - cooked and sliced
1 cup milk
2 slices jalapeño pepper - then minced
2 eggs or equivalent Egg Beaters™
1 cup flour
salt and pepper to taste
1 tablespoon butter or margarine

Preheat oven to 400°. Place sausage slices in a greased baking dish - a glass pie plate works great. Prepare batter (mix together the rest of the ingredients) in a bowl. Pour batter over sausages and bake uncovered for 30 minutes until puffed, crisp, and golden brown. This comes out spectacular so if you are trying to impress someone make sure they are there when it comes out of the oven. *This will deflate much like a soufflé.

Our tobaccco barn near the Chemung River burned down in 1956 after being struck by lightning. Almost the same location as the photo on the opposite page.

Who says a collie dog can't drive a tractor? Here is my Grampa and a collie dog at the wheel of a brand new 1920 Massey-Ferguson tractor - sold to us by Mr. Harry Ferguson in person. Photo below is the same location in 2006.

Quiche Diane – No Crust
Like me

½ cup deli ham - chopped

3 eggs (or equivalent Egg Beaters)

1 cup milk

1 cup shredded cheese – gruyere, fontina, cheddar or combination

½ cup bread crumbs

1 cup chopped vegetables (you may do one kind or go crazy and mix a bunch - I like broccoli, of course, but sometimes corn, carrots, tomatoes, peppers, onions - just so it's 1 cup's worth

1 teaspoon Italian spices

1 teaspoon dried parsley or 2 tablespoons fresh

1½ teaspoons butter or margarine

Salt and pepper to taste

Preheat oven to 375°. In mixing bowl, beat eggs, and add other ingredients. Pour into greased baking pan. Bake uncovered for 30 – 45 minutes until bubbly and top is browned, and when inserted toothpick comes out clean.

A crust just adds more fat, and who needs that? Not me.

For any recipe in this book that calls for milk you really can use whatever you like - whole, skim, soy, cream, half & half, or fat-free half & half. Any recipe that calls for butter you may easily substitute margarine. We prefer no trans fat margarine like Olivio.

Cheesy Wieners & Potatoes

Sounds like 1960 - but it tastes good!

3 medium potatoes - sliced
2 hotdogs or soy dogs - sliced (we like fat-free hotdogs)
8 mushrooms - sliced
1 small onion - diced
½ pound broccoli or asparagus - chopped
1 can Campbell's Cheddar Soup plus ½ can milk or cream
Tabasco to taste
1 teaspoon minced garlic
¼ cup grated parmesan cheese (low-fat is good)
Dash of white wine
1 tablespoon olive oil
One good pinch of your favorite herb or spice (thyme, rosemary, Italian spice, Creole spice, curry, etc)

1. Preheat oven to 350°. In pan, sauté onions with a little olive oil. Add mushrooms and broccoli or asparagus. Cook slightly. Put aside in bowl. Next sauté or boil potatoes until they are "almost but not quite" cooked. Mix potatoes with other vegetables in bowl.

2. Cheese sauce: Empty the cheddar soup into a mixing bowl. Add milk and white wine, stirring until well mixed. Add olive oil, and your spice and stir. Grease a casserole dish and add potatoes, hotdogs, and vegetables. Pour sauce over all. Sprinkle parmesan cheese over and bake uncovered until brown and bubbly about 30 minutes.

Above - Don't worry - the tractor wasn't moving. My father "working" the controls and a puppy deciding which direction to go, circa 1930. The house in the background was my Uncle Fritz's on the Brand Flat Road. It was originally built around 1820 for John Kline, the ferry boat pilot who operated a ferry across the Chemung River in the area of today's Brand Park.

Right, my father and his wheelbarrow and one of our many smaller greenhouses, also circa 1930.

Meat

The back of this photograph says, "These are the little fellows. The pen is where the old green house used to be. Its pretty hard to get a good picture. Henry was afraid you wouldn't know how many there are so I was to tell you there are four little ones." Photo circa 1920.

Boeuf Bourguignon

Or if you make it with hamburger we call it

Hamburguignon

1 cup red wine
5 tablespoons fresh parsley - minced
1 teaspoon dried thyme or 1 sprig fresh thyme
1 bay leaf
1 clove garlic - minced
2 tablespoons oyster sauce
1 pound stew beef or ground beef
Flour to coat the meat (or ¼ cup to mix with the ground beef)
1 onion - minced
1 tablespoon tomato paste
6 tablespoons butter or margarine
2 cups beef stock
2 carrots - cut in thick slices
1 teaspoon Dijon or Creole mustard
Dash red pepper flakes
10 baby portobella mushrooms – sliced
Salt and pepper to taste
Hot cooked potatoes or rice to serve this over – or you can even do the way we do it on the farm and serve over bread. Mmmmm!

Roll meat in flour (except if you are using ground beef). In a big pot, brown the meat with the butter, or margarine. If using ground beef, sprinkle flour on the meat after its browned and stir.

Add everything else. Cover and let cook over medium-low heat for 30 to 45 minutes, or as long as you can stand it. Salt and pepper to taste. If it needs to be thicker: mix 2 teaspoons corn starch with 4 teaspoons cold water. Add a little at a time until its thick enough. Serve over potatoes, rice, or bread. Remember what your mother said, "Don't eat the bay leaf."

Above, irrigating cabbage the hard way. The person whose face you can't see (farthest left) is probably my Grampa, then Uncle Fritz and Uncle Gus, circa 1935.

Below, my Uncle Fritz standing next to the pole barn (where today is our next door neighbor's backyard).

Miss Diane's Louisiana Boudin (boo-dan) (Pork & Rice patties)

A really good homemade sausage

First,

1 onion - chopped finely

2 celery ribs - chopped finely

½ green or red pepper - chopped finely

1 clove of garlic - chopped

In a small pan with a little olive oil and water, sauté these ingredients about ten minutes. Remove from heat and mash.

Then, in mixing bowl add above cooked ingredients and the following:

1½ lbs. ground pork (or even what the stores sell as meatloaf - beef, pork, veal combo - works great)

Handful fresh chopped parsley

2 eggs – scrambled (or the equivalent Egg Beaters™)

½ teaspoon oregano

½ teaspoon white pepper

½ teaspoon black pepper

½ teaspoon cayenne pepper

½ teaspoon garlic powder

1 teaspoon poultry seasoning

2 teaspoons sage

Creole spices (Tony's™ is perfect) or salt to taste

1½ cups cooked rice

Mix together thoroughly and form patties. Fry slowly in a little olive oil and a little water (these tend to be drier than hamburgers and need some moisture in the pan) until brown. Don't flip too soon as they need to be brown to stay together. Enjoy as a breakfast sausage, or have on a bun like a hamburger, or with a side of greens.

Southside Goulash
A traditional favorite

½ pound tomatoes - diced, or one 14 oz. can diced tomatoes -
drained
2 tablespoons butter or margarine
¼ onion - diced
ground beef (about 2 hamburgers worth)
3 tablespoons flour
¾ teaspoon hot paprika
salt and pepper to taste
½ cup water optional
½ teaspoon raw sugar
hot cooked egg noodles (we like No Yolks™)

Sauté onion in butter. Brown ground beef in onion pan add flour and maybe a little water if beef is lean. Add paprika, salt and pepper, sugar, and tomatoes. Cover and simmer 1 hour. Add some water if necessary. Serve over egg noodles.

We started using raw sugar after our first trip to New Roads, Louisiana. Raw sugar is made using cane sugar from the initial pressing of the cane, allowing the natural molasses to remain in the crystals. The flavor is sweet and rich. The color is natural amber.

Chile con Chicken
Good for nachos, too

1 chicken breast - diced

1 onion - chopped

1 clove of garlic – minced

½ tablespoon of chili powder

salt and pepper to taste

1 teaspoon cumin

1 teaspoon dried oregano

½ teaspoon Hershey's

chocolate syrup – come

on give it a try

McIlhenny's Tabasco to

taste

1 pound fresh diced

tomatoes or 1 can (14 oz.)

- drained

1 can (14 oz.) your choice

of beans

¼ cup water

salt and pepper to taste

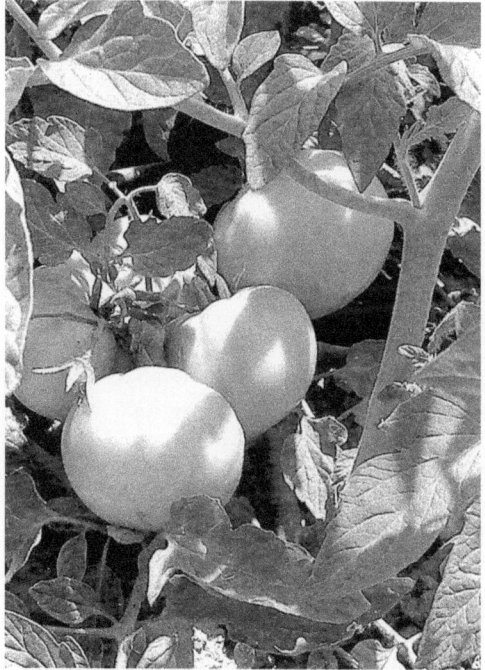

Young tomatoes, 2005.

In big pot cook meat, onions and garlic until meat is done. Add all ingredients except for beans. Bring to boil – then cover and reduce to simmer for one hour. Add beans. Season to taste. Simmer 10 more minutes. Serve with corn chips and sour cream. 2 servings.

Young peppers growing in the sunshine, 2005.

Janowski's South of the River Chili

½ pound ground beef or diced chicken
½ pound chorizo or andouille sausage - sliced
2 teaspoons chili powder
2 teaspoons cumin
2 teaspoons dried oregano
1 teaspoon minced garlic
dash cayenne pepper powder
1 each - diced hot pepper, green pepper, red pepper, onion, and carrot
5 mushrooms - sliced
3 tomatoes - seeded and chopped
¼ cup corn
½ cup cooked rice
½ bottle of your favorite beer - you may drink the rest!
1 (8 oz.) can tomato sauce and 3 cans of water
1 can of beans - your choice but I like the big white ones
Salt & pepper to taste
sour cream, shredded cheese, tortilla chips
Extra cayenne, tabasco, cumin, cilantro if you want

In a big pot, brown meat. Add tomato sauce and water. Add dry herbs/spices. Add vegetables (except beans), rice, and beer. Bring to boil. Add salt & pepper. Cover and simmer 1 to 1½ hours stirring occasionally. Add beans during last 15 minutes. Serve with tortilla chips and sour cream on the side.

Vegetarians, you might want to look away. We did grow our own meat. Pork and cabbage were staples in German diets - for some of us they still are! I must admit that I do love boiled cabbage.

Our farm stand on Esty Street in 2005.

Farm Style Pot Roast

1 nice piece of meat – your choice of roast about 2 pounds
Salt and pepper to taste
Flour to roll meat in
2 cups beef broth
1 clove garlic - minced
2 carrots – sliced
2 ribs celery – sliced
1 onion – diced
½ cup beer
4 diced potatoes
2 teaspoons cornstarch mixed in small bowl with 2 tablespoons
water
olive oil

In big bowl roll meat in salt, pepper, and flour. In a big pot with some olive oil – brown meat on all sides. Add beef broth, beer, and vegetables – except potatoes. Bring to a boil, then medium-simmer covered for 1 hour - turning occasionally. Add potatoes. Potatoes will be done in about 20-30 minutes. If at the end of cooking the gravy isn't thick enough for you – just mix in corn starch/water a little at a time to the gravy while mixing to thicken it. Salt and pepper to taste.

I always thought this was my Uncle Fritz but up close in Photoshop it's my Grampa - sometimes its hard to tell - he and his brothers look very similar. Photo circa 1925. Note the smokestack on East Church Street in the background.

Chili CORN Carne

I put corn in everything - even pizza

1 red onion - diced
1 hot red pepper - diced
1 Anaheim pepper - diced
1 green pepper - diced
½ pound meat- your choice ground beef, chicken, or sausage
12 small mushrooms - sliced
12 cherry tomatoes - whole or crushed
1 cup corn - yes, it gives a nice crunch
1 tablespoon of chili powder
1½ teaspoon cumin
1½ teaspoon dried oregano
1 tablespoon minced garlic
1 (8 oz.) can tomato sauce plus 1 can of water
1 can white beans
Olive oil
Salt and pepper to taste
Sour cream and tortilla chips

In a big pot, sauté onions, peppers, meat, and tomatoes with a little olive oil and water. Add the garlic, cumin, oregano, tomato sauce and water. Bring to a boil, then add the mushrooms and corn, cover and reduce to simmer for 20 minutes. Season to taste. Add the beans then simmer 5 minutes more.

If you have the time to spare – this will taste better if you let it simmer for an hour or so. It lets the flavors blend together really well.

Pointe Coupée Chicken

Denny and I are part-timers in Pointe Coupée Parish, Louisiana. We do a lot of historical work down there - check out our website - www. pcatm.org. This recipe has been adapted from one of my favorite cookbooks - *Mandy's Favorite Louisiana Recipes* by Natalie Scott.

2 chicken breasts

2 tablespoons butter or margarine

5 small onions

4 tablespoons of flour dissolved in 4 tablespoons water

10 baby portobella or brown mushrooms - sliced

2 cups chicken broth

½ teaspoon parsley

½ teaspoon thyme

Salt, pepper and cayenne pepper to taste

1 egg yolk mixed with 1 tablespoon lemon juice in a small bowl

Hot cooked rice or potatoes to serve over

In big pot, brown chicken breasts in butter. Sauté mushrooms and onions in a small separate pan then add to big pot. Add chicken broth, herbs, salt and pepper, and spices, and bring to a boil, cover and reduce to simmer about 20 minutes. Add half of the flour/water mixture to thicken. Stir and after a few minutes if its not as thick as gravy should be just add more of the flour/water and stir.

Remove a big spoonful of the gravy into the small bowl with the lemon juice and egg yolk and mix well. Return this mixture to the big pot and stir well. Simmer for a few more minutes to cook the egg. This recipe makes a nice gravy - serve over rice or potatoes.

Gyros
Very Good

2 pita breads

¼ cup plain yogurt

½ teaspoon dried mint

½ teaspoon sugar

1 small pickle cucumber - grated

ground beef - about one hamburger's worth

¼ teaspoon cumin

¼ teaspoon oregano

salt and pepper to taste

1 clove garlic - minced

½ teaspoon onion powder

1 tablespoon olive oil

1 cup shredded lettuce

1 tomato - seeded and chopped

Brown the ground beef and remove from heat. In mixing bowl, mix yogurt and herbs and spices. Season to taste. Add tomato, pickle, meat, and lettuce. Split pitas halfway and stuff mixture into pocket. Enjoy.

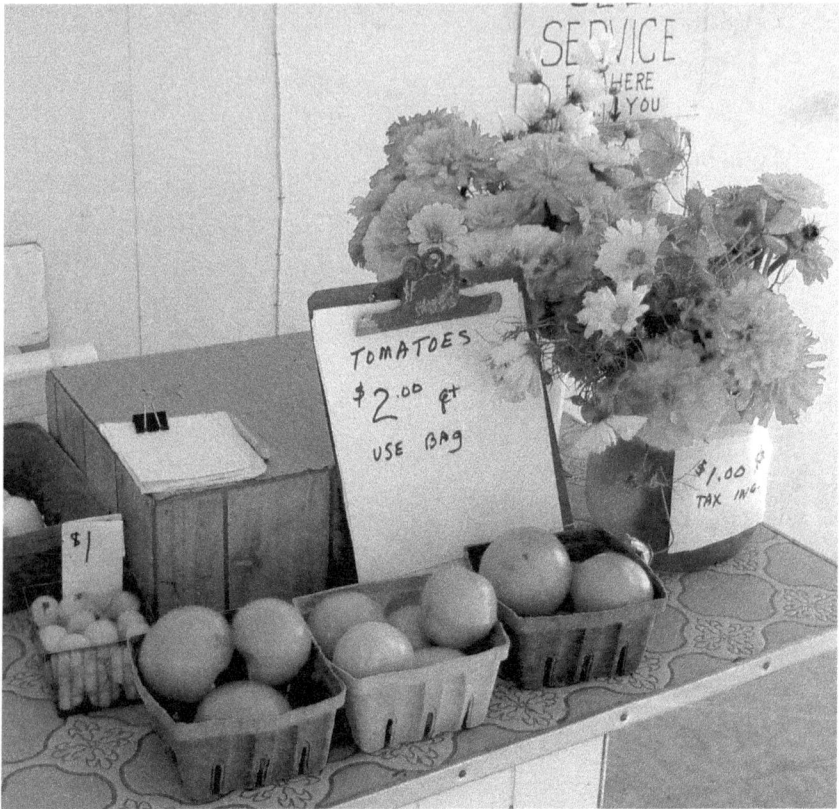

Fresh tomatoes and flowers for sale in our farm stand on Esty Street. Below - cucumbers in baskets, 2005.

Seafood and Poultry

This isn't about fish - it's about swimming in the Chemung River.
Nice bathing suits circa 1920. Aunt Anna is third from the left.

Crawfish or Chicken Etoufée (ay-too-fay)

OK, I know it's hard to find crawfish in the North so you could sub-stitute shrimp or chicken. This is sort of a vegetable, gravy, and meat over rice dish.

1 pound cooked crawfish tails, shrimp, or diced chicken

Green part of one green onion - sliced

½ yellow onion - chopped

¼ bell pepper - chopped

2 ribs celery - sliced or shredded

1 tablespoon olive oil

2 cloves garlic - chopped

8 tablespoons butter (1 stick) or margarine

2 tablespoons cornstarch dissolved in 1 cup vegetable broth

¼ cup minced fresh parsley - this is the secret to good etoufée

Black pepper

Red pepper

Salt

Hot cooked rice

In big pot, sauté chopped onion, bell pepper, celery and garlic in but-ter until onions are clear. Add cornstarch/broth to pot and cook until thickened. Add parsley, crawfish tails (chicken or shrimp) and sea-sonings and heat thoroughly. Serve over hot rice and garnish with the green onion. Serves 2 hungry people.

Crab Burgers

Like Crab Cakes only meatier

2 egg whites

1 small can crab meat

¼ cup grated cheddar or mozzarella (fat-free works great too)

¼ teaspoon dried dill

Minced green onion or onion powder to taste

¼ cup mayonnaise

½ cup bread crumbs or fresh bread cubes

2 tablespoons ketchup or your favorite barbecue sauce

Old Bay™ seasoning to taste

garlic powder to taste

dash of Worcestershire sauce

3 teaspoons sweet pickle juice - just open the pickle jar in your fridge

1 tablespoon minced celery

1 teaspoon lemon juice

Tony's Creole Seasoning or salt and pepper to taste

1 teaspoon minced jalapeño

Mix the first 4 ingredients together. In a small bowl, combine the rest of the ingredients and then add them to the crab mixture. Make burgers. Fry in pan. **Don't flip these until the "down side" is brown – they'll stay together better. Fry in pan until brown enough for you.

Here is Uncle Henry who lived next door. You can see the field behind him and the Chemung River levee before it was raised, circa 1935.

Below, Uncle Gus stands amongst the cabbages. Uncle Gus built the house that my parents live in today.

Stuffed Fillet of Tilapia

(or any thin fish)

Better than at a restaurant. This is our all-time favorite fish.

4 tilapia fillets - same size
4 tablespoons butter or margarine - melted
salt and pepper

Stuffing:

4 tablespoons butter or margarine
2 slices of onion - finely chopped
1 rib celery - finely chopped
5 mushrooms - finely chopped
½ red or green bell pepper - finely chopped
½ clove garlic - minced
1 tablespoon flour
¼ cup white wine
¼ cup milk
6 oz. (½ can) crabmeat or shrimp
¼ cup bread crumbs
pinch of dried oregano
1 tablespoon fresh parsley - chopped
1 egg white or Egg Beaters™
4 tablespoons parmesan cheese - grated (low-fat is great)
salt, pepper, and paprika to taste

Preheat oven to 375°. Spray 13x9 baking dish with non-stick pan spray.

Sauté onion, celery, pepper, garlic and mushrooms in butter until tender. Blend in flour. Add wine and cream and stir until thick. Remove from heat and set aside for a moment.

Stuffing: In mixing bowl add remaining ingredients (except paprika) and mix well. Add sautéed vegetables and mix. Season to taste with salt and pepper.

In baking dish spread 2 tablespoons olive oil across bottom. Lay two bottom fillets down and spoon a ½ inch layer of stuffing over each, place top fillet over. Sprinkle top of fish with melted butter and paprika and bake partially covered 30 - 45 minutes, or until bottom fillets are done. The thicker the fish, the longer it needs to bake.

More wood to be chopped. Uncle Fritz, circa 1935.

JFK's Chowder

I have been on 3 Kennedy pilgrimages. Once I went to Boston on a Shortline bus just to go to the Kennedy's favorite restaurant (the Union Oyster House) and have a bowl of clam chowder - nearly 800 miles round trip for soup. It was worth it! This recipe has been adapted from the *White House Cookbook.* You can make it with fish, clams, lobster or crabmeat.

½ pound cooked or canned fish, clams, lobster or crabmeat

¼ cup water

½ onion - chopped

1 potato - cooked and diced

¼ cup celery - chopped

1 bay leaf

vegetable bouillon powder or salt and pepper to taste

2 cups milk

1 tablespoon butter

½ cup clam broth

Sauté onions and celery. In pot add seafood, potato, onions, celery, bay leaf, bouillon or salt and pepper, clam broth, milk and butter. Simmer covered 5 minutes. Serves 2.

For any recipe in this book that calls for milk you really can use whatever you like - whole, skim, soy, cream, half & half, or fat-free half & half. Any recipe that calls for mayonnaise or sour cream you may easily substitute low-fat, no- fat or soy versions. We do like Olivio margarine for a buttery flavor with no trans fats.

"The Path - Buttonwoods" by prominent Elmira photographer Charles Van Aken in 1906 on, or near, our property. Buttonwoods are more commonly known as sycamores. "The Buttonwoods" is the name of our neighborhood on the Southside from Maple Avenue along the river to Luce Street and named for the huge trees. The neighborhood was populated by mostly Germans and Irish in the late 19th and early 20th centuries. There are still some beautiful buttonwood trees in Brand Park near the swimming pool. We have one on our farm.

Grampa on a horse next to our levee, circa 1910. My great-great grampa Frederick built this little levee on our property probably right after he purchased the property - many years before the state built the big one. This one still exists in our woods.

Too fuzzy to tell who the two people in the back are, but a nice photo of our greenhouse, circa 1910.

Uncle Gus with a horse in what is today my parents' backyard looking southeast.

Creamy Lime Chicken
Impressive

Marinade:

1 cup water

¼ cup teriyaki sauce

2 tablespoons fresh lime juice

2 teaspoons minced garlic

¼ teaspoon liquid smoke flavoring

½ teaspoon salt

¼ teaspoon ground ginger

4 chicken breasts

Prepare marinade by combining ingredients. Add chicken. Cover and refrigerate 2 hours.

Dressing:

¼ cup mayonnaise

¼ cup sour cream

2 teaspoons tomato paste

1½ teaspoons balsamic vinegar

1 teaspoon minced jalapeño pepper

1 teaspoons minced onion

¼ teaspoon parsley

Tabasco to taste

salt and pepper to taste

dash dry dill

dash paprika

dash cayenne pepper

dash cumin

dash chili powder

dash garlic powder

black pepper to taste

Prepare dressing by combining ingredients. Mix until smooth.

Preheat oven to 350°. In pan, brown chicken breasts in a little olive oil.

Arrange cooked chicken in baking pan. Spread dressing on tops. Bake uncovered 20 minutes or until sauce is bubbly.

For any recipe in this book that calls for milk you really can use whatever you like - whole, skim, soy, cream, half & half, or fat-free half & half. Any recipe that calls for butter you may easily substitute margarine. We prefer no trans fat margarine like Olivio.

Chicken and Vegetable Alfredo
An excellent alfredo

½ pound bow-tie or any fun time pasta

1 cup of your choice of vegetable

2 tablespoons butter or margarine

1 chicken breast – diced

Alfredo Sauce

2 tablespoons butter or margarine

1 tablespoon corn starch mixed in a little bowl with 2 tablespoons cold water

salt and pepper to taste

1 cup milk

vegetable bouillon powder (enough to season ½ cup liquid)

¼ cup grated parmesan cheese (low-fat is great)

1 teaspoon minced garlic

Splash of white wine

Pinch of basil

Pinch of parsley

Three things happen at same time – you do need to think about timing.

1. In small pan, sauté the chicken in the butter until done. Add the veggies and sauté a few minutes more. Then add milk, corn starch/water, salt, pepper, and bouillon. Bring to a slow boil and keep stirring so it doesn't stick on the bottom.

2. In big pot cook the pasta. Drain.

3. When everything is ready, combine all in the big pot, add the cheese and serve.

Casseroles or Hot Dishes

(one of my favorite movies is "Fargo")

Cousins Harold Loop, on left, and Mildred
Schiller, circa 1916.

Farmers' Market Vegetable Casserole

A contemporary casserole - no mushroom soup involved

Steamed on the bottom - cheesy and crisp on the top

1½ pounds potatoes (white or red) - sliced thin

½ onion - sliced thin

1 medium zucchini - cut into ¼ inch pieces

2 carrots - sliced thin

1 tablespoon fresh or dried thyme

1 teaspoon fresh or dried marjoram

Salt and pepper to taste

½ cup dry white wine or water

3 tablespoons butter or margarine

1 cup French or Italian bread cubes

2 cups grated cheese cheddar or mozzarella (fat-free is good)

Preheat oven to 375 °.

Layer vegetables in a greased casserole dish in the order listed. Sprinkle with herbs, and salt and pepper as you go. Pour wine (or water) over all. Cover with foil and bake for 45 minutes. Melt the butter in small pan. Add bread cubes and stir until they absorb the butter and get a little crispy. Remove from heat. Uncover the casserole and spread the cheese, then layer the bread over the top. Continue baking **uncovered** until the cheese melts and the bread cubes have browned about 10 more minutes. Serve and enjoy. Serves 3 or 4.

Hearty Tuna or Crab Noodle Hot Dish

Something in this cookbook was going to be called a Hot Dish and this might as well be it. Ja, you betcha.

1 can chunk-style tuna or crab

3 cups uncooked egg noodles (we like No-Yolks™)

½ cup celery - chopped

¼ cup green onions - sliced

½ cup sour cream (fat-free works too or plain yogurt)

1 teaspoon Dijon or Creole mustard

½ cup mayonnaise

½ teaspoon fresh or dried thyme

salt and pepper to taste

1 small zucchini - sliced

1 cup shredded monterey jack or mozzarella cheese - can be fat-free

Optional: 1 medium tomato - seeded and chopped

Optional: chopped fresh parsley, dill, basil or chives

Preheat oven to 350°. Drain and flake the tuna or crab. Set aside. Cook noodles according to package directions. Drain and rinse in hot water. In bowl, combine noodles with tuna, celery and green onions. Blend in the sour cream, mustard, mayonnaise, thyme, cheese, and salt and pepper. Spoon mixture into a buttered casserole. Bake uncovered for 30 minutes or until hot and bubbly. When finished - sprinkle with the chopped tomato, parsley, dill, basil or chives.

Left is my grandmother, Loretta, down by the river. Photo dated May 29, 1927. My grandma worked in our farm stand for many years.

Fruit

My cousin Pauline (Walker) has the right idea
about dessert here - watermelon in the sunshine,
circa 1933.

Cornfield in 2006.

Strawberry Scone Bisquits
Tastes like springtime

2 cups flour
2 tablespoons sugar
2 teaspoons baking powder
½ teaspoon baking soda
½ teaspoon salt
¼ cup softened butter or margarine
½ cup milk
1 egg (or 2 egg whites) or equivalent Egg Beaters™
½ pint strawberries sliced

Preheat oven to 475 °. Grease cookie sheet. Combine flour, sugar, baking powder, baking soda, and salt in large bowl. Beat milk and egg in small bowl. Pour onto dry ingredients and stir. Add strawberries and stir. Knead lightly.

From a spoon (or even using 2 spoons) drop bisquit-size portions onto cookie sheet. Bake 10-14 minutes until golden brown. Serve warm. Makes 8 to 12 large bisquits.

Nothing like cooking outdoors - this photo is a few days after the 1972 flood - in the background the barns still have 2 feet of water (high water was up to the ceiling on the first floor). Here is my father and my brother, Tom, cooking something in our driveway - we had no electricity, gas, heat, or telephone service for many days. I don't remember what they were cooking, but there is a big steaming pot of water on the ground.

The best breakfast I ever ate was the morning after we returned home after the flood (we were refugees) when my Grampa made blow-torched eggs made by heating the bottom of a frying pan with a blow torch. That recipe is too dangerous to repeat in this cookbook so just use your imagination.

Fresh Fruit Sorbet

Delicious and refreshing - This is a nice dessert that you can make without any special equipment - just a small plastic container that is shakeable.

1 cup water
½ cup sugar
1 cup pureed fresh fruit - your choice

In small pot, bring water and sugar to a boil. Lower heat and simmer 5 minutes. Remove from heat. Add fruit and stir. Put mixture into a plastic freezer container (we use a clean one-pound margarine tub) that is slightly bigger than quantity of mixture. (Foods expand during freezing and if the container is too small there will be a freezer catastrophe). Put container into freezer.

**Shake container every 30 minutes to break up the ice crystals until completely frozen – about two hours – otherwise you'll have a frozen hockey puck not sorbet.

Another alternative is to make this in a Donvier ice cream maker. They are great - no salt or electricity. Takes about 15 minutes.

I don't know who these people are - but they are enjoying a round of croquet in what is now my parents' backyard on Esty Street, circa 1910.

Grampa's Elderberry (or Anyberry) Pie

My Grampa gave me an elderberry bush and I pick its berries every August and make myself a pie.

1¼ cups sugar

¼ cup flour

dash salt

3 cups elderberries or any kind of berries

1 10-inch pie shell

1 egg white

5 tablespoons vanilla, plain, or berry flavor yogurt (no-fat is fine)

¼ teaspoon cinnamon

1 teaspoon corn starch dissolved in 3 teaspoons water in a small bowl

Preheat oven to 450°. Mix together sugar, flour, salt, elderberries, yogurt, cinnamon, and corn starch/water combination. In the pie shell add the egg white and swish it around so it covers the inside of the shell. Hold on to the shell and tip it over the sink to remove the excess eggwhite. Eggwhite helps to keep the shell from getting soggy. Pour in fruit mixture. Bake at 450° for 20 minutes – then reduce heat to 325° and bake for 30 minutes more.

Elderberries are an acquired taste. They have a bitterness to them. The yogurt helps.

Strawberry Pecan Ambrosia

It certainly is! Great as a dinner dessert or a breakfast energy burst

2 cups pineapple - drained - you can drink the juice - it's good for
you

4 cups of orange sections - chopped roughly

1 cup fresh shredded coconut

1 cup sliced strawberries

1 cup coconut milk or substitute 1 cup cream (can be fat-free) mixed
with 4 teaspoons powdered sugar

3 tablespoons fresh lime juice

1 cup chopped bananas

Dash brandy if desired

½ cup Louisiana pecans - or find the best you can

Combine fruits, coconut milk (or cream), brandy, and juice. Just before
serving top with pecans.

Above, Aunt Anna sits on the front porch with two young suitors on a beautiful day, circa 1920.

Below, Aunt Anna with a friend. View looking east down Esty Street, circa 1920.

Index

Diane Janowski is a local history writer in Elmira, New York and publisher of *New York History Review*. She has been actively involved in the history of Chemung County, New York since 1979, including serving as the former editor of the *Chemung Historical Journal*. She co-authored the book *Images of America: The Chemung Valley* with Allen C. "Denny" Smith. Janowski and Smith have also worked on an extensive historical photographic documentary in Pointe Coupée Parish, Louisiana called *Pointe Coupée at the Millennium* - www.pcatm.org.

Please visit these websites

www.NewYorkHistoryReview.com
www.JanowskiGardens.com

www.ingramcontent.com/pod-product-compliance
Lightning Source LLC
Chambersburg PA
CBHW032105080426
42733CB00006B/431